The
Travel Doodle
Book

Published in 2009 by Prion Books
An imprint of the Carlton Publishing Group
20 Mortimer Street, London W1T 3JW

Images copyright © 2009 Ross Adams
Design & layout copyright © 2009 Carlton Publishing Group

A CIP catalogue record for this book is available from the
British Library

ISBN 978-1-85375-721-1

Printed in Dubai

10 9 8 7 6 5 4 3 2 1

THANK YOU

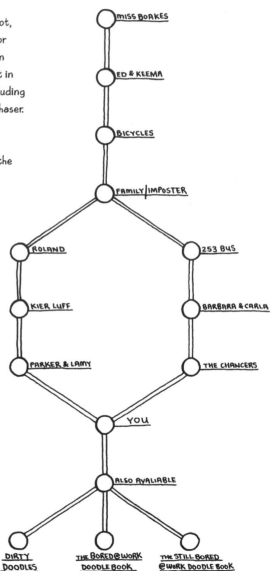

MISS BOAKES
ED & KEEMA
BICYCLES
FAMILY / IMPOSTER
ROLAND
253 BUS
KIER LUFF
BARBARA & CARLA
PARKER & LAMY
THE CHANCERS
YOU
ALSO AVAILABLE
DIRTY DOODLES
THE BORED @ WORK DOODLE BOOK
THE STILL BORED @ WORK DOODLE BOOK

The Travel Doodle Book

ROSE ADDERS

PRION

Draw in this book

Colour in the images

Fill in the drawings

Stick things in it

Fill the pages while you're waiting

Cover the pages in idle thoughts

It's your book... use it!

Who is doing the hard work?

Complete the free paper spread (with lots

THE FREE PAPER

| MINOR CELEBRITY SEEN DRUNK: | FILM STAR LOOKS PERFECT AGAIN: | STAR SIGN |

| CHOCOLATE ADVERT: | NEW TV SERIES ADVERT: |

| | FAST FOOD ADVERT: |

THEATRE ADVERT:

COFFEE ADVERT:

NEW BEST SELLING BOOK ADVERT:

PAGE NUMBER:

of pretty pictures)

SPORT:

FOOTBALLER'S WIFE SPOTTED IN A BIKINI:

ARTIST PAID MILLIONS FOR BAG OF AIR:

JOBS

WORLD NEWS:

DIET PLAN ADVERT:

HOME ENTERTAINMENT ADVERT:

CHEAP FLIGHTS ADVERT:

COSMETIC SURGERY ADVERT:

ANOTHER NEW TV SERIES ADVERT:

PAGE NUMBER:

Make a comic strip based on what the loud person is talking about

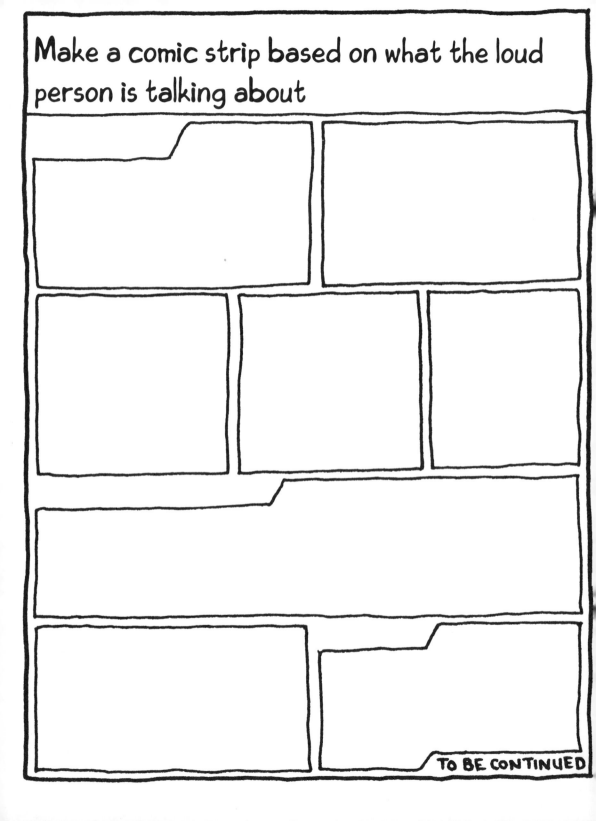

TO BE CONTINUED

What will you grab to stop yourself moving when they slam on the brakes?

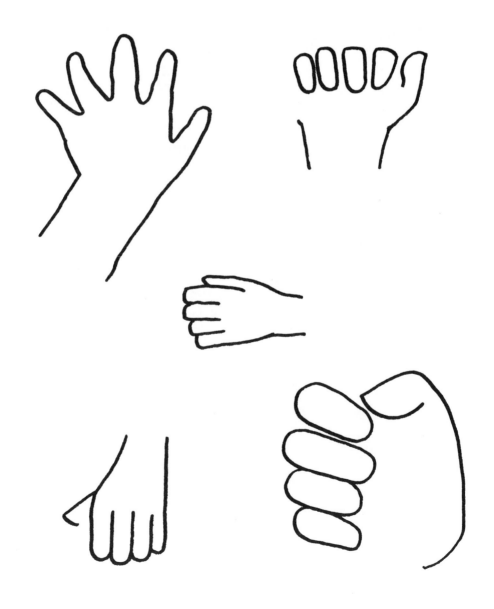

Destination picker: close your eyes and let your pen guide you

MOUNTAIN | SOUTH AMERICA | RESTAURANT | WISHING WELL

WORK | DENTIST | PUB | BEACH | ISLAND | PARK | HILLS

HOME | HEAVEN | FESTIVAL | ? | VISIT OLD FRIEND | SHOPS

:) | NORTH | WWW. | BERMUDA TRIANGLE | MIAOW

OVER THERE | PLACE OF EXERCISE | PIER | JUNGLE | CLUB

CENTRAL TRAVEL POINT | LAKE | GYM | SCHOOL | DESERT

AUSTRALIA | BAR | ROUND THE CORNER | NUMBER 23 | MARKET

WHERE EVERYBODY KNOWS YOUR NAME | PARTY | HOTEL | NEAREST BRIDGE | BED

STAY WHERE YOU ARE | LIBRARY | NEXT DOOR | WAR ZONE

CASTLE | GIG | UPSTAIRS | EUROPE | FRIDGE | BANK | B+B

VISIT THE SHAMAN | WORK | PUB | SHOPS | COAST | EAST

FOREST | POOLSIDE | HOME | HOSPITAL | ASIA | DESK | ME

HAUNTED HOUSE | ART GALLERY | TIMBUKTU | TREEHOUSE

STOP | SOFA | PLACE OF HISTORIC INTEREST | BACKSTAGE

WEST | BAR | AFRICA | VISIT FAMILY | X | HOME | NEST

OVER HERE | GOING DOWN | BATHROOM | HELL | WORK | BOAT

FOLLOW THE BREAD CRUMBS | SPACE | FIELDS | CAFÉ | CAPITAL | DARK ALLEY | CAVE

BIKE SHEDS | TOILET | BACK IN TIME | ANTARCTICA | DOCTOR

VISIT ELDERLY | DOG HOUSE | MUSEUM | CHEAPEST FLIGHT

PLACE OF WORSHIP | NORTH AMERICA | STADIUM | END OF THE ROAD

? | THE MOON | PUB | 1984 | CLIFF | MOTEL | STUDY THE BROCHURE

BEACH | THE RUINS | SOUTH | ROOF | BOOKIES | UTOPIA | RIVER

FAVOURITE CHAIR | MY WAY | CANAL | HELP OUT | POST OFFICE

SLUMS | VISIT PARENTS | PARK | END OF THE RAINBOW | SUN

WORK | HOME | RIOT | GO BACK! | ATLANTIS | DOWNSTAIRS

MIND (what's in?) THE GAP

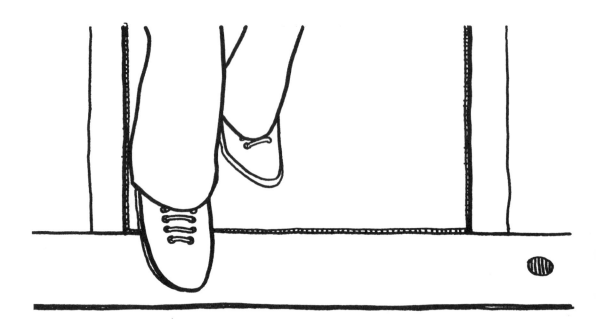

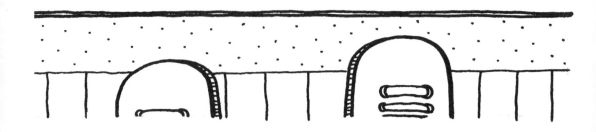

MIND (what's stuck in?) THE DOORS

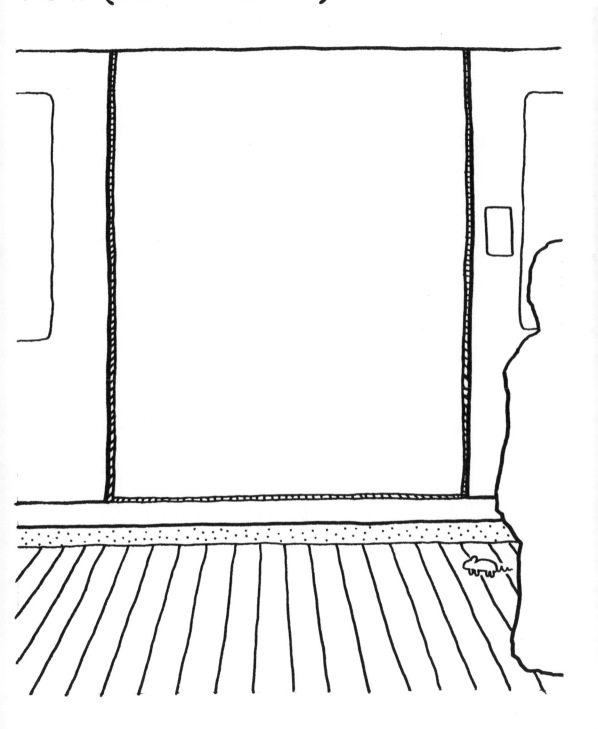

What will you see through your sunglasses?

What a load of bollards

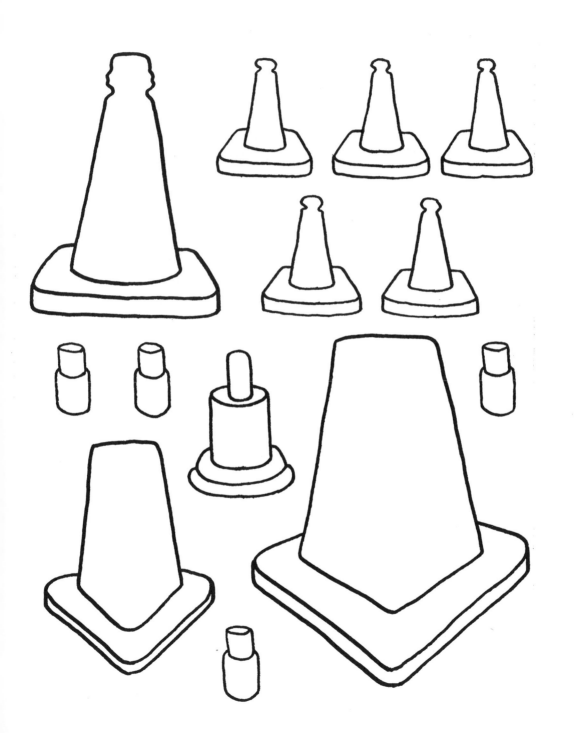

Design a rollercoaster that travels faster than sound

Design a pram for adults

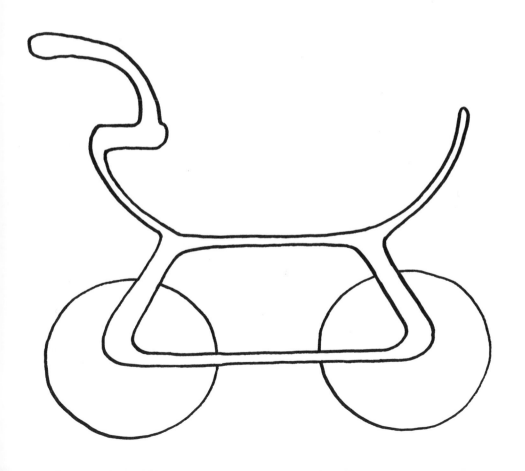

Get from A to B

A

B

Add reins and saddles to these trusty steeds

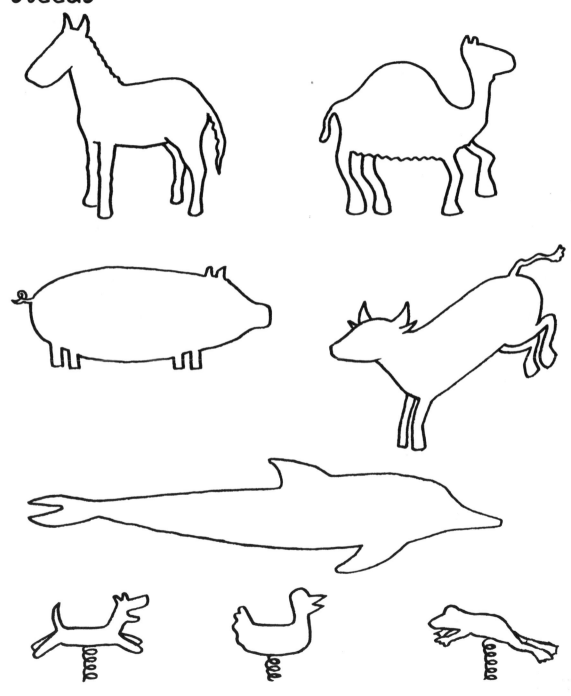

Add the barriers to the check-in queue

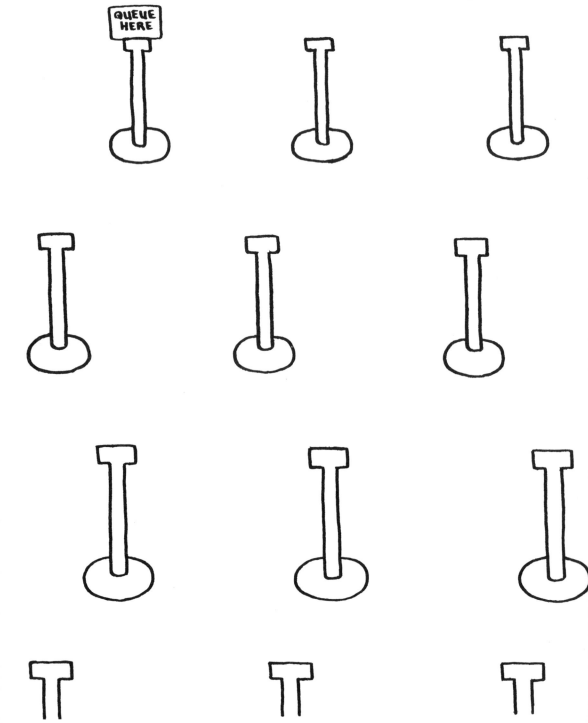

What changes did you make to the Park n' Ride sheme?

Identify the roadside food

What do you eat at thirty thousand feet?

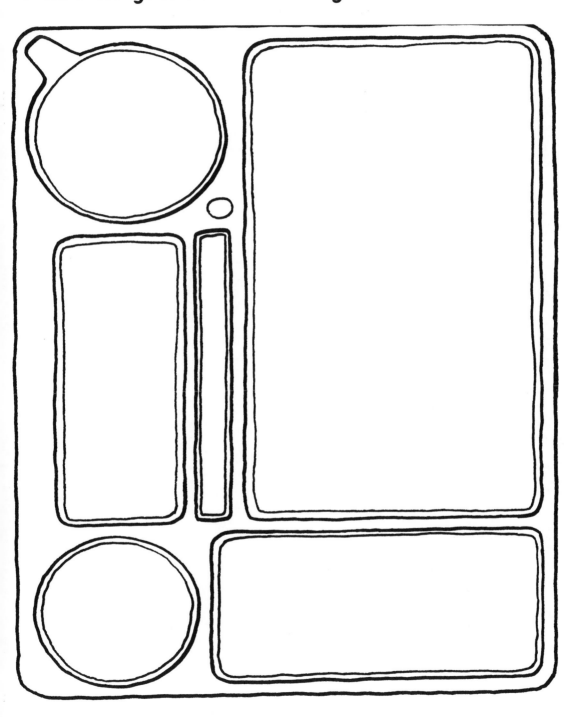

Close your eyes, rest your pen on a start
point and let the travel motion draw
 for you

① ② ③

④ ⑤ ⑥

⑦ ⑧ ⑨

⑩ ⑪ ⑫

Make some short journeys on the underground

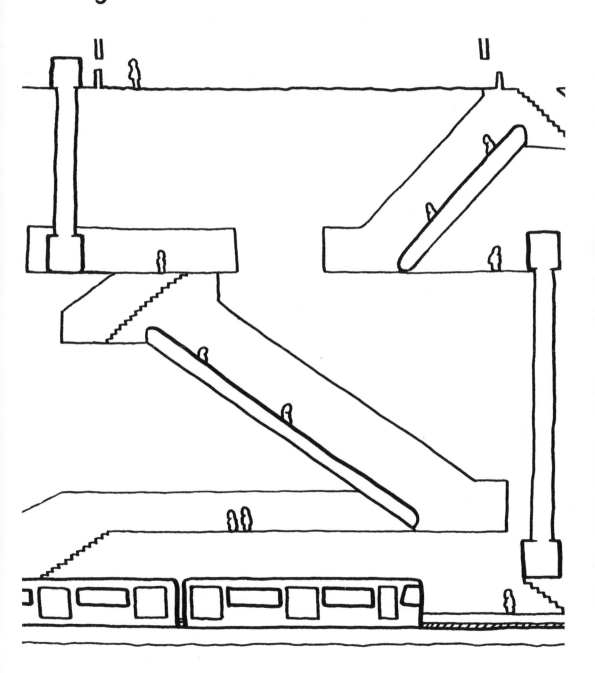

Draw some interesting plumage for the migrating birds

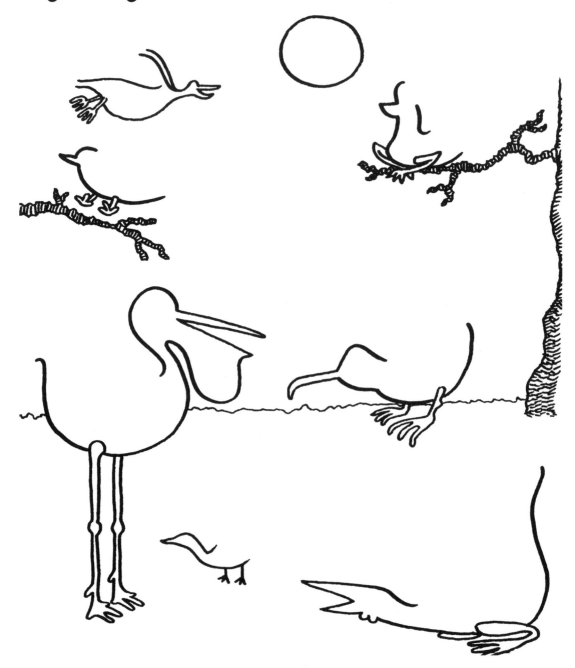

What did they leave out of the picture in the fancy hotel brochure?

What did Dave find while exploring the coastline?

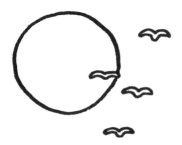

What has caused panic on the beach?

Complete the map of your ideal travel

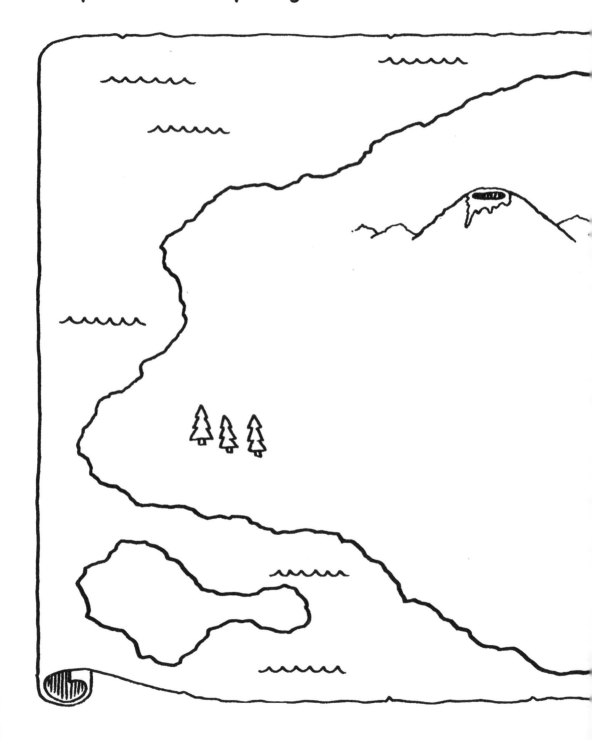

destination

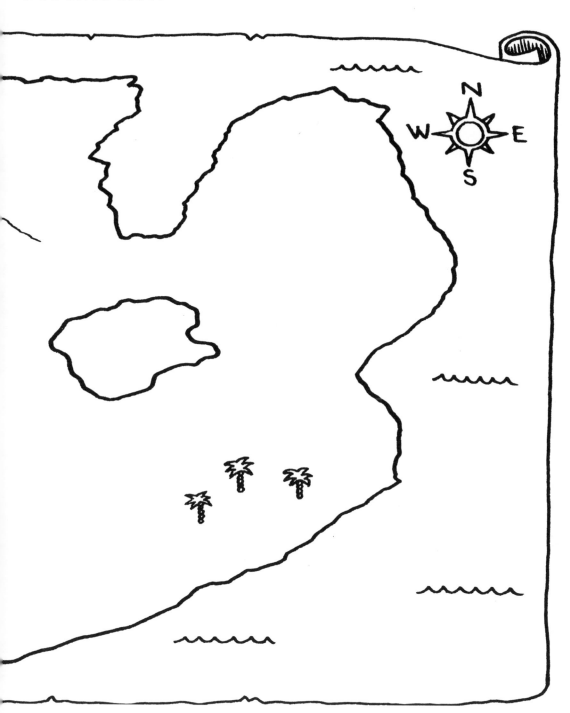

Don't get locked out!
What keyring will you not forget?

Complete the contour lines of this unexplored terrain

Add some extra stars and identify your own formations to navigate from

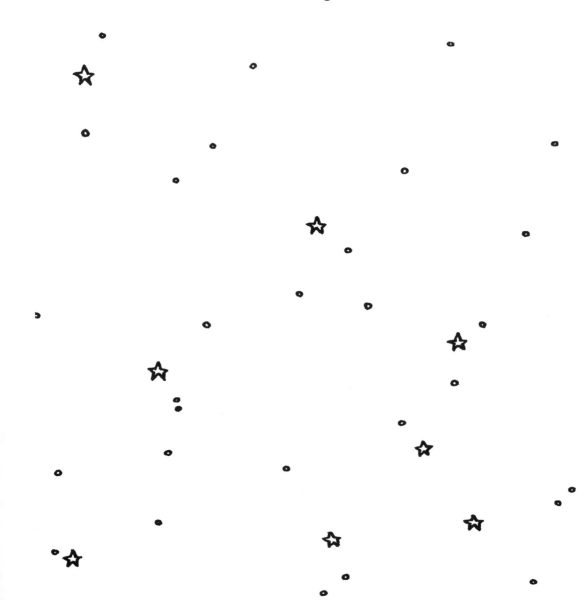

Design the ultimate machines to conquer air, land and sea...

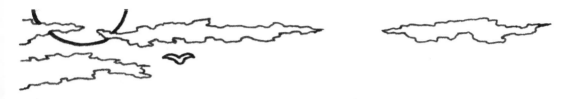

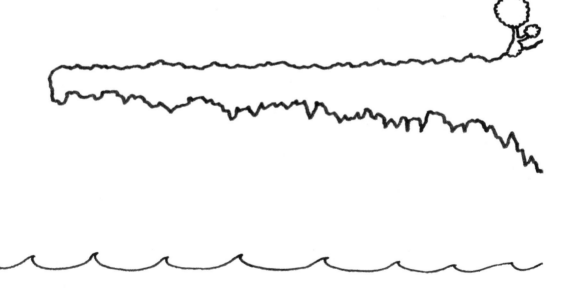

Will you help or hinder Dave's way back to safety?

Stop overnight: fit everyone else in the tent

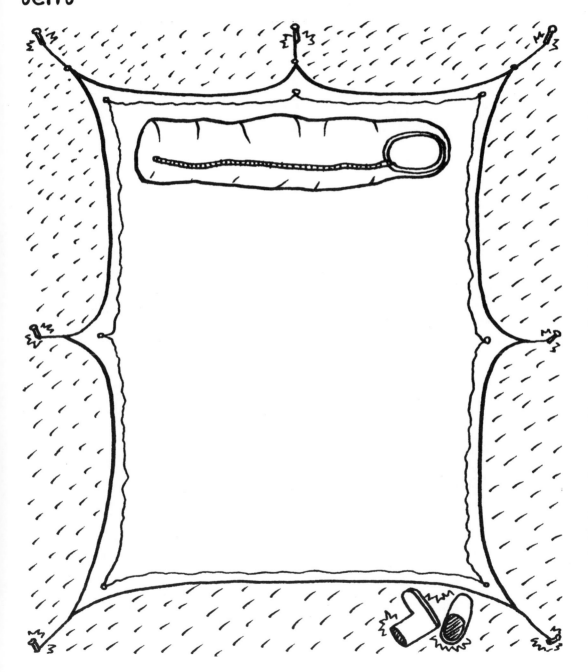

Draw new landmarks for each area

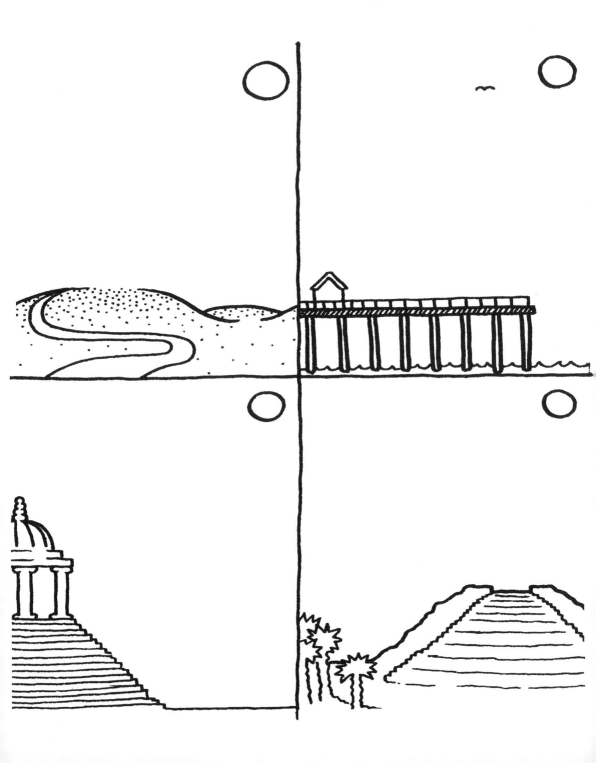

Draw people cooking on the sun-loungers

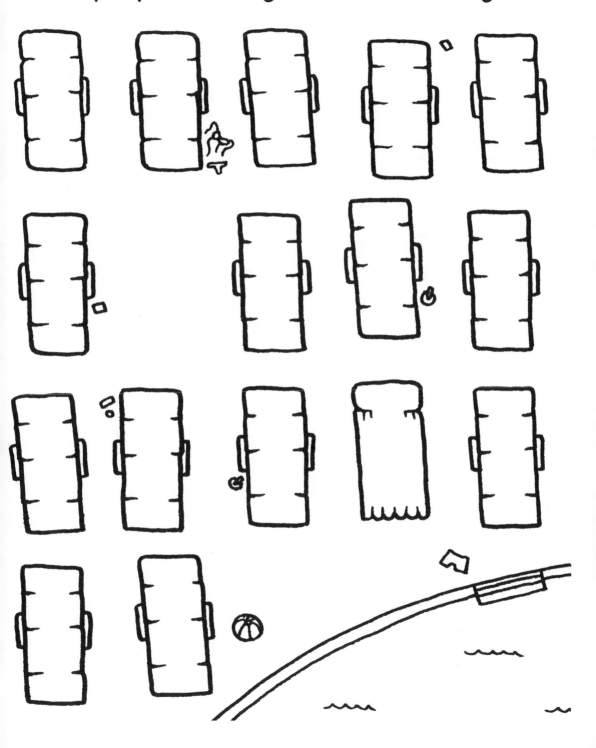

Can you remember what is buried in each layer of your rucksack?

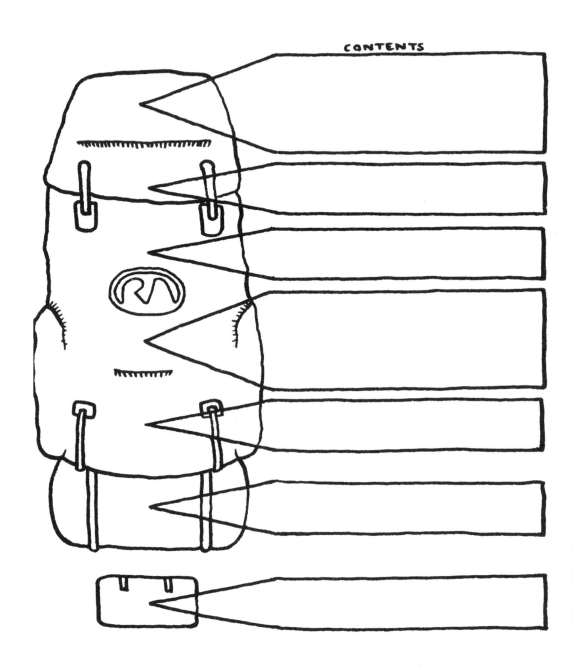

CONTENTS

Put some sand between these toes

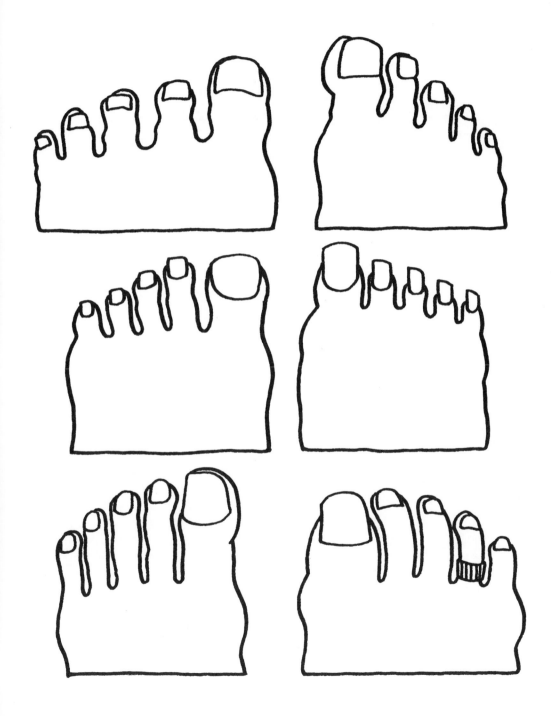

What can you see from the summit?

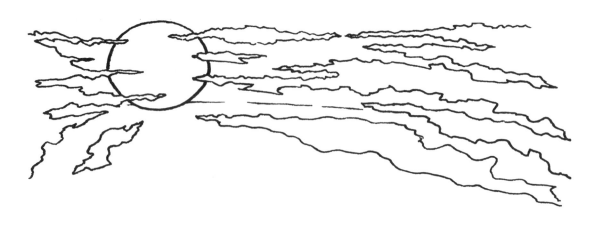

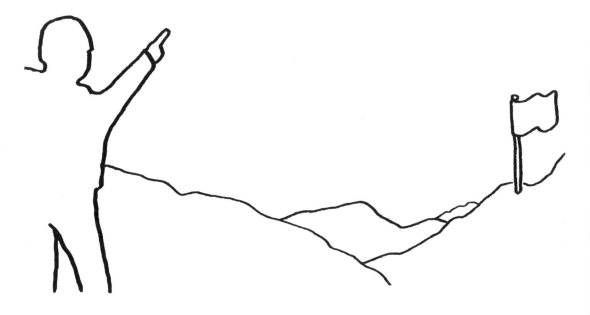

Make your bags easier to spot in baggage collection

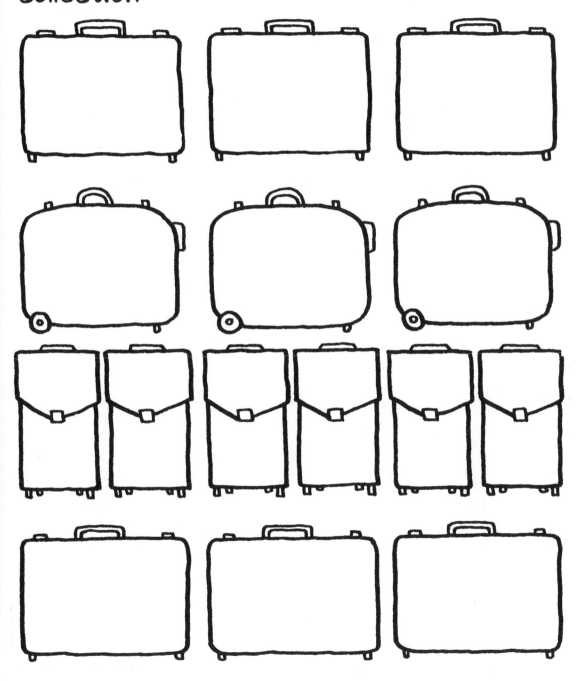

Design some special holiday cockroaches

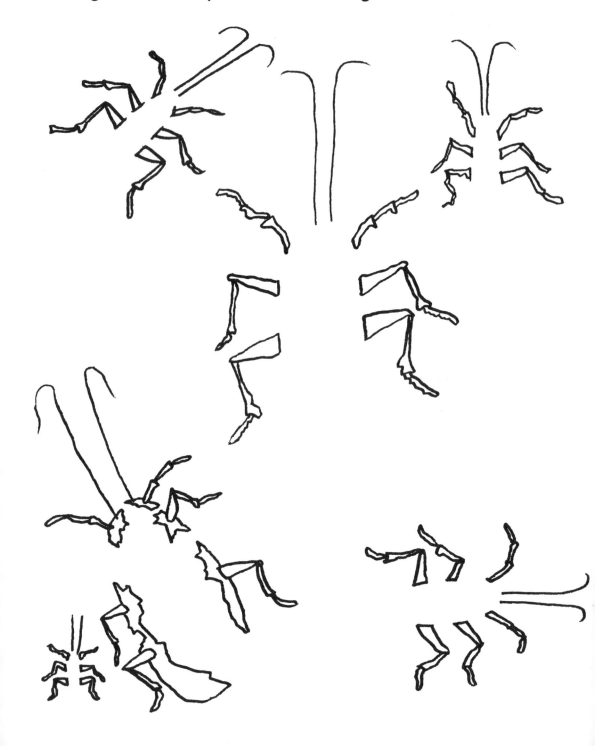

....and their queen!

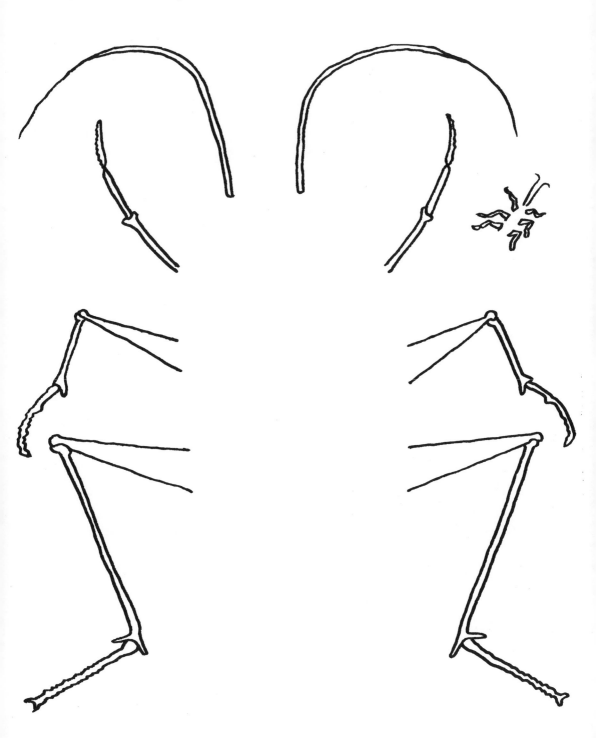

Send some bungee jumpers over the edge

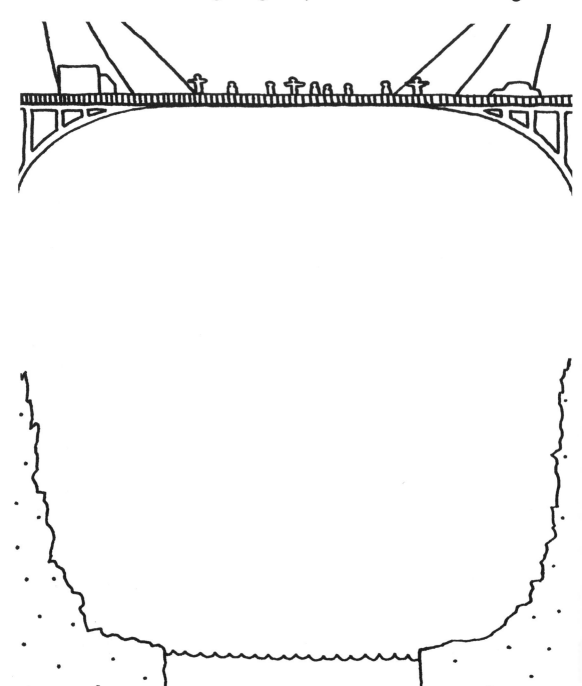

Draw bugs all over the speeding truck

Complete the passport photos....

.....and x-ray their hand luggage

Complete the new motorway service signs

Still waiting for the number 9 bus?

Draw your toothbrush relaxing at home

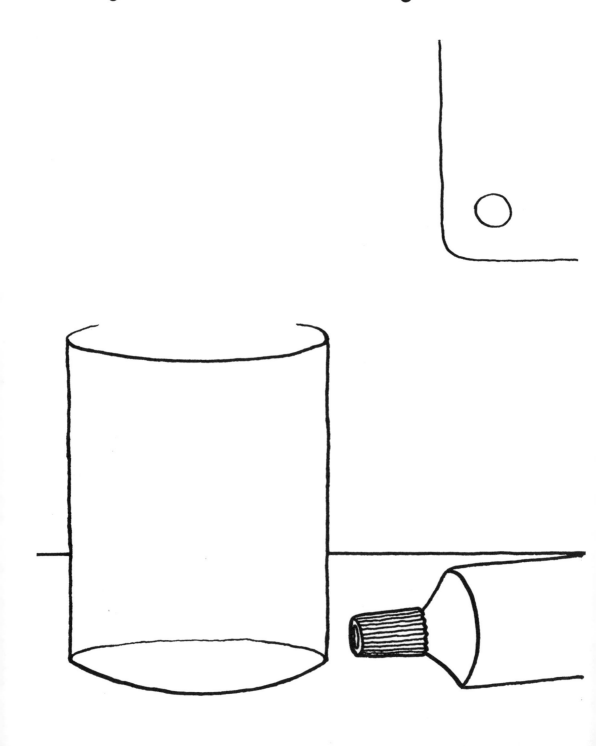

Complete the gestures of the road

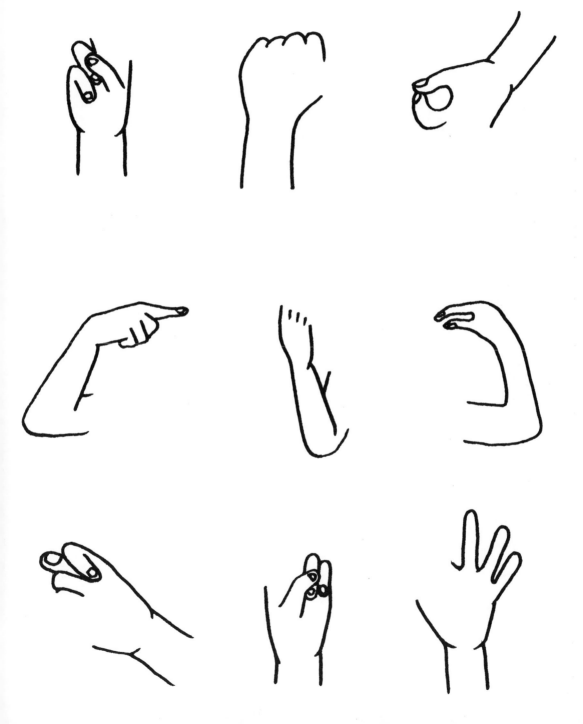

What has come off the back of the lorry and caused a jam?

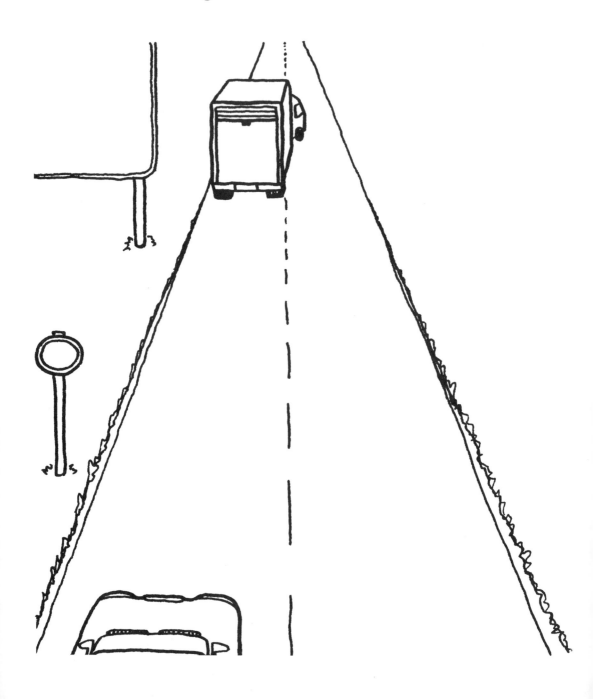

What is the SAT-NAV saying?

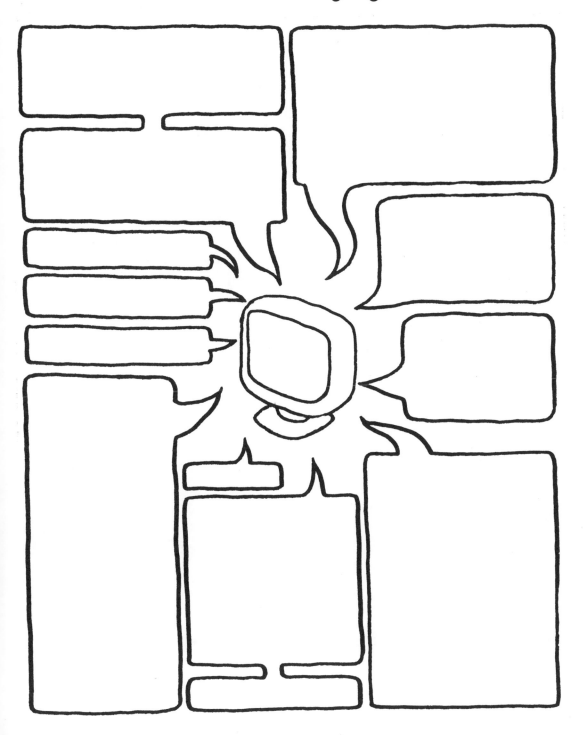

Pimp these rides

What does the traffic update board say?

Complete cards for your cab firm dream

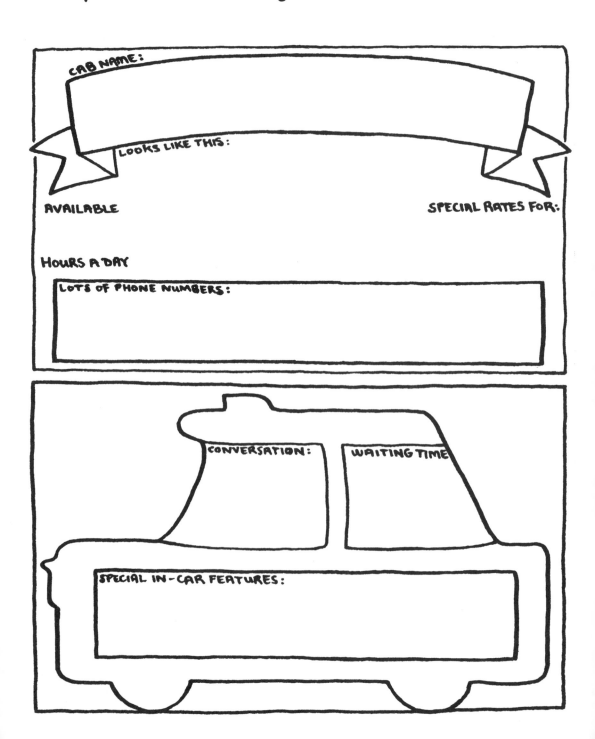

CAB NAME:

LOOKS LIKE THIS:

AVAILABLE

SPECIAL RATES FOR:

HOURS A DAY

LOTS OF PHONE NUMBERS:

CONVERSATION:

WAITING TIME

SPECIAL IN-CAR FEATURES:

Play seat spotter

WHERE?

RUBBISH?	CHECK ☐	DAMP?	CHECK ☐
COMFORT?	CHECK ☐	FREE PAPER?	CHECK ☐

LENGTH OF STAY?

WHERE?

RUBBISH?	CHECK ☐	DAMP?	CHECK ☐
COMFORT?	CHECK ☐	FREE PAPER?	CHECK ☐

LENGTH OF STAY?

WHERE?

RUBBISH?	CHECK ☐	DAMP?	CHECK ☐
COMFORT?	CHECK ☐	FREE PAPER?	CHECK ☐

WHERE?

RUBBISH?	CHECK ☐	DAMP?	CHECK ☐
COMFORT?	CHECK ☐	FREE PAPER?	CHECK ☐

Take part in the mobility car 4x4 rally...

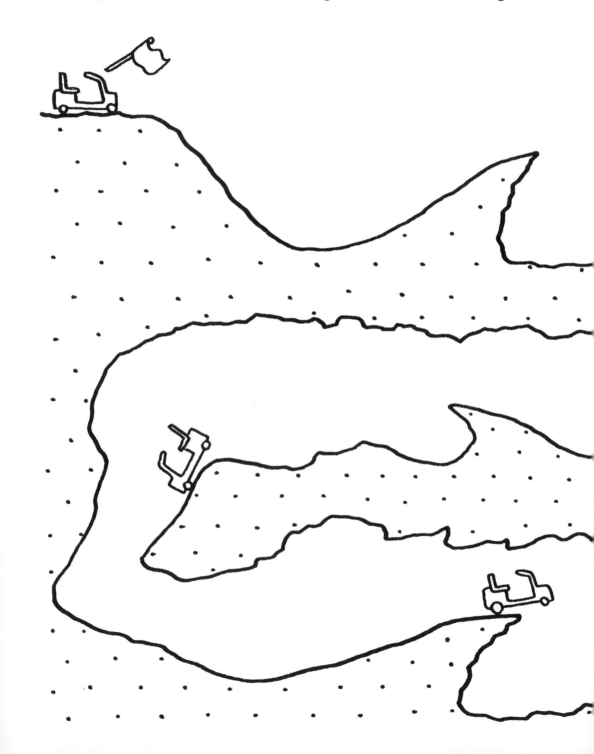

... but don't drop your shopping

What are the roadworks really for?

Trail these flights with (carbon) footprints in the sky

Add bodies to the roadkill

Trapped in the carriage with a mysterious foul odour? Draw arrows to indicate the possible sources

What do you see on the scenic route?

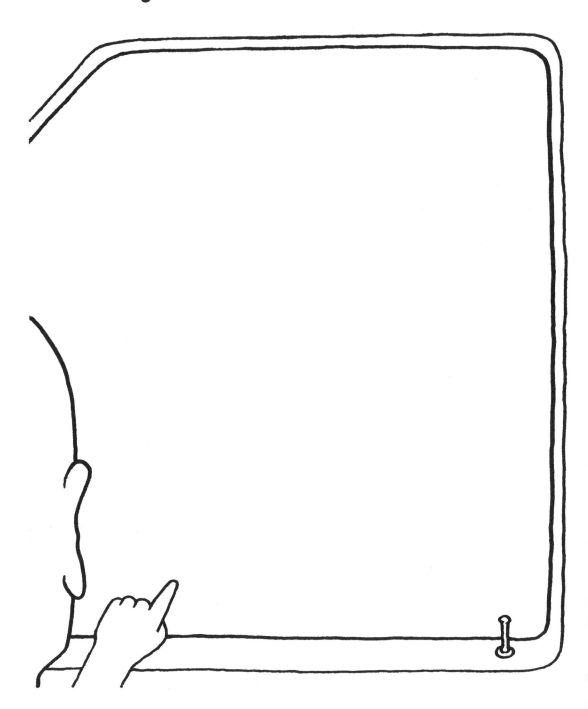

Can you remember what the air hostess told you to do?

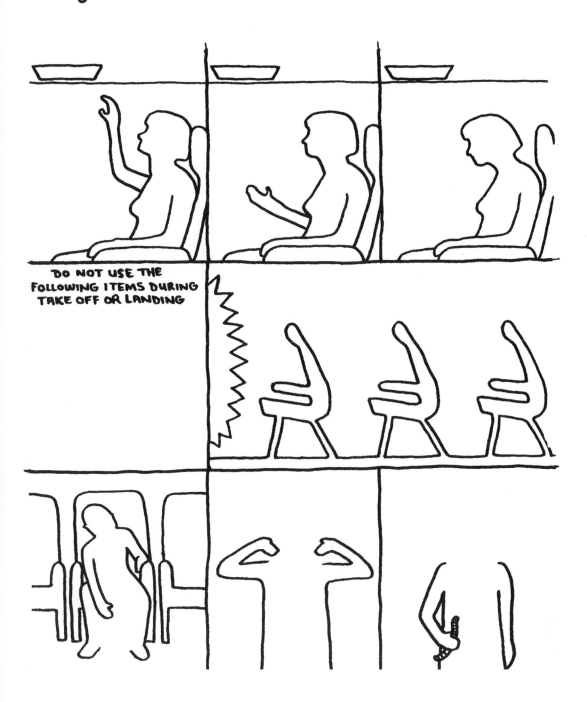

Design an upgrade for this first class seating area

Complete your dodgy souvenir shopping list

①

②

THIS IS A _____

IT IS FOR _____

THIS IS A _____

IT IS FOR _____

③

④

THIS IS A _____

IT IS FOR _____

THIS IS A _____

IT IS FOR _____

⑤

⑥

THIS IS A _____

IT IS FOR _____

THIS IS A _____

IT IS FOR _____

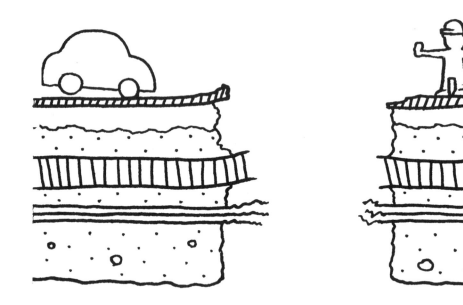

Double up with duty-free double vision

Predict the next traffic lights

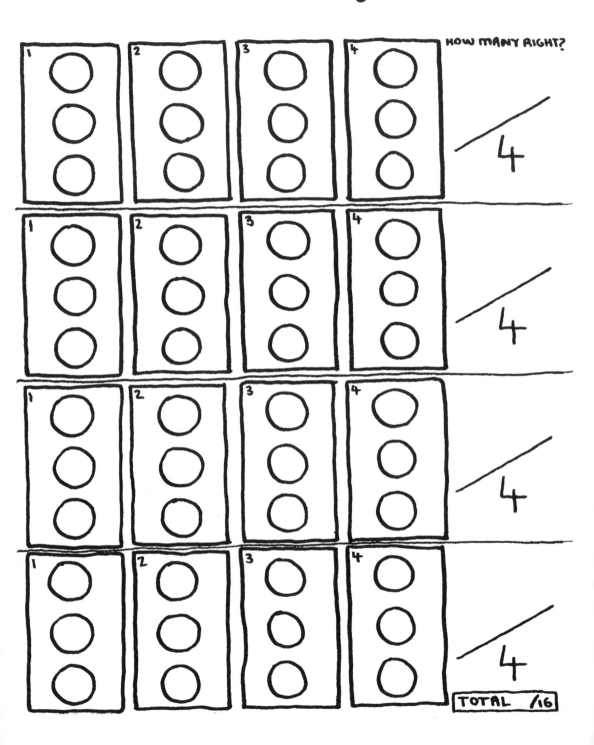

HOW MANY RIGHT?

/4

/4

/4

/4

TOTAL /16

How do you know this isn't your hotel room?

Travel sickness: try to contain it

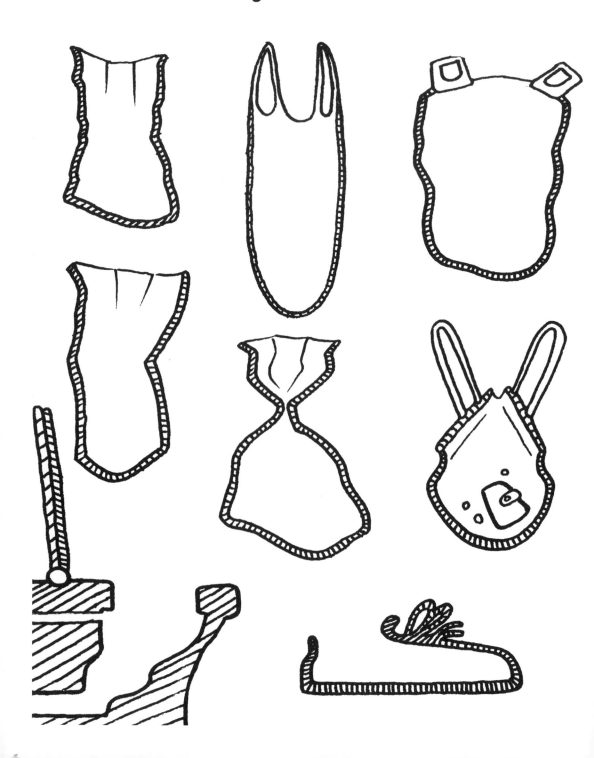

What's in Dave's back seat?

Make these forms of travel extreme

Clamp the traffic wardens

Give these travellers lots of hot air

Get stuck next to the 'weirdo'

You decide where the bus stops

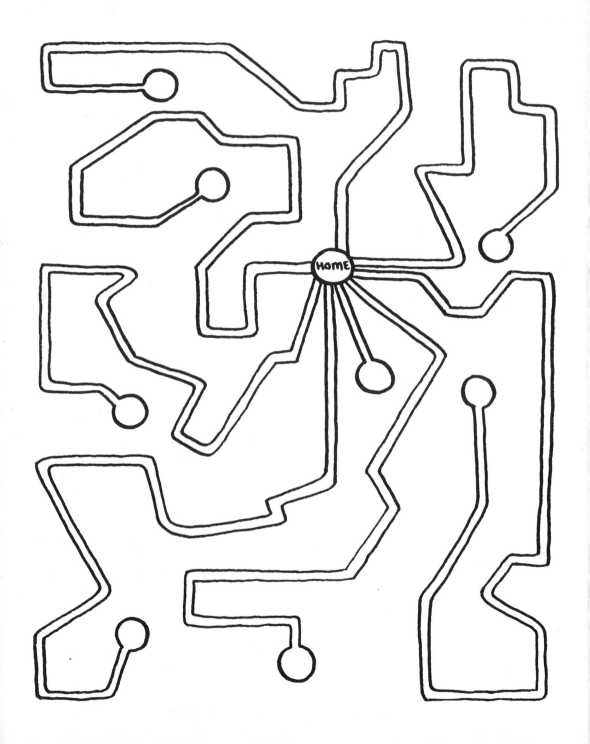